HOW TO LIVE LIKE

A VIKING

WARRIOR

Thanks to the creative team:
Senior Editor: Alice Peebles
Designer: Lauren Woods and collaborate agency

Original edition copyright 2015 by Hungry Tomato Ltd.

Hungry Tomato™
A division of Lerner Publishing Group, Inc.
241 First Avenue North
Minneapolis, MN 55401 USA

For reading levels and more information, look up this title at www.lernerbooks.com.

Main body text set in Century Gothic Regular 10/13.
Typeface provided by Monotype Typography

Library of Congress Cataloging-in-Publication Data

The Cataloging-in-Publication Data for *How to Live Like a Viking Warrior* is on file at the Library of Congress.

ISBN 978-1-4677-6354-7 (lib. bdg.)
ISBN 978-1-4677-7213-6 (pbk.)
ISBN 978-1-4677-7214-3 (EB pdf)

Manufactured in the United States of America
1 – VP – 7/15/15

HOW TO LIVE LIKE A VIKING WARRIOR

By Anita Ganeri

Illustrated by Mariano Epelbaum

HUNGRY TOMATO™

Minneapolis

Being a Viking warrior can be
tiring work. Don't forget to stock
up on sleep whenever you can:
all that fighting and feasting can
take its toll.

Contents

The Viking Warriors

It's the year 905. You've traveled back in time to a Viking village on the shores of southern Norway. The long, cold winter is over and everyone's busy getting ready . . . to go raiding. Join us if you dare.

Olaf Sharpaxe at your service, son of the local **jarl** (earl). Rich pickings of gold and treasure from raids have made my father very wealthy. The only person more important is the king (as my dad's fond of telling everyone). But never mind about all that. The really brilliant news is that I'm now old enough to go raiding this summer with my father and brothers for the first time.

I CANNOT WAIT!

WARNING!

Being a Viking warrior isn't for everyone. You need to be brave and tough. If you don't think you've got what it takes, stick to your farming and stay at home.

Who are the Vikings?

You've ended up in Norway, but Vikings also live in Denmark and Sweden. From here we head off to faraway places, in search of plunder, land, and trade. Vikings are famous for being fierce warriors, and it's true. But we're also brilliant shipbuilders, clever craftsmen, and accomplished poets. You'll just have to take my word for it.

Norway

Sweden

Denmark

If you're going to be a Viking warrior, you'll need a suitably scary name. Choose something fierce-sounding like Bjorn ("bear"), Ulf ("wolf"), or Thorvald, after Thor, the hammer-throwing thunder god.

Training for Raiding

Being a warrior is a top job in Viking society, and it's all I've ever wanted to do. My father gave me my first sword when I was only two years old. It was made of wood, but I still had some good fights with my friends. When I was ten he gave me my first iron weapons: a sword, a shield, and an ax. Since then I've been training hard every day. My dad keeps a band of warriors as bodyguards, and they've been showing me how it's done. Today's the last day of training before we set off on the raid.

WARNING!

If your father isn't a jarl, you'll have to work even harder to be picked for a raid. Grab every chance to practice fighting, look willing, and you might be in luck.

In our village, you have to be old enough to be picked for a raid. Luckily, I had my birthday last month.

How to stay fit, Viking-style

In between raids, trainee warriors need to stay in shape and show fighting spirit. The best way to do this is by playing sports. Don't pick a sport like football or basketball: they're for wimps. Real Vikings opt for things like wrestling, archery, and throwing the javelin (spear).

1 Archery is excellent for developing your hand–eye coordination. It's also a handy way to catch something for dinner.

2 Spear-throwing builds upper-body strength and sharpens your competitive edge. After all, you don't want be beaten by Ulf or Thorvald.

3 Wrestling allows you to be aggressive, which, for a Viking, is a good thing. It's also about endurance. How long can your strength hold out against your friend's?

Joining the Hird

Most of the men in our village aren't full-time warriors. They're farmers who join up in summer to sail off on the jarl's raids. If you want to become a professional, you need to join a **hird** (a band of men who fight for a jarl).

As part of the hird, you'll live in the jarl's household, eating and sleeping in his hall. You won't get your own bedroom. You'll have to grab one of the benches by the wall. Try and get as close to the fire as possible.

WARNING!

If you don't like your hird, you can leave without any loss of honor. But you'll have to wait until the new year.

A hird has a strict pecking order. The closer you sit to the jarl at the feasting table, the more important you are. So it's bad luck if you need the bathroom and lose your place.

How to swear an oath of loyalty

When you join a hird, you swear an **oath** of loyalty to the jarl and your fellow warriors. Your oath lasts until you die, so it's a deadly serious undertaking.

1 You swear your oath on a sacred silver arm ring, colored red with blood.

2 In return for your loyalty, the jarl promises to look after you and reward you with jewelry, land, and weapons.

3 If you betray your jarl, all your land and belongings are taken away, and you'll be declared an outlaw. The other warriors then swear to kill you.

4 You'll suffer the same fate if you hurt a fellow warrior with your fists or with weapons.

Setting an Example

"You're only as good as your leader," my father's always saying, and there are plenty of Viking warriors from the past to serve as your role models. For years, I've heard stories of their cunning, strength, and derring-do. Take Erik Bloodaxe, for starters.

One of the most famous Vikings ever, brutal Erik Bloodaxe definitely lived up to his bloodthirsty nickname. Leaving a trail of destruction behind, he murdered both of his brothers to become king of Norway. Clearly a fearsome warrior, he was also horribly violent and was lucky enough to have good **skalds** (poets) to put a better spin on his dubious deeds.

Ragnar Lodbrok

Young Ragnar Lodbrok ("hairy-breeches") fought off his rivals to become king of Denmark. He then went off raiding until his luck finally ran out. On his last raid in England, Ragnar was captured by the king of Northumbria and thrown into a pit of snakes to be bitten to death. He died singing about his exploits. What a guy!

Olaf Tryggvason

Olaf Tryggvason learned about raiding the hard way. His family was captured by Vikings in eastern Europe, and he was sold as a slave in exchange for a cloak. Rescued by his cousin, he became a top warrior in the guard of the king of the Rus, in the land that would eventually become Russia. Later, he raided in Denmark, Sweden, and England, and he could juggle three knives at a time. He made so much money that he was able to become the king of Norway.

Weapons and Armor

If you're going to be a vicious Viking, you need to look the part. The most important parts of a warrior's kit are his weapons: get the best you can afford. Ideally, you'll have a spear, a sword, and a battle-ax. There are different spears for stabbing and throwing, and you'll need to master both. There are two kinds of axes: the single-handed ax and the two-handed broadax. Axes are big and heavy, so give yourself plenty of room to swing. This is when all that fitness training really pays off. Sling your shield over your shoulder while you're swinging, so it protects your back.

What to wear

The best thing to wear into battle is a chain-mail shirt, called a **byrnie**. It's made from thousands of iron rings welded together. Chain mail's expensive (my dad passed his old shirt on to me), but it could save your life. You'll also need a helmet, made from metal or leather, and a shield. Choose one made from wood and leather, with a leather or metal rim.

Give your sword a fierce-sounding name, such as Leg Biter, Stone Biter, or Adder. It'll show your enemies that you mean business.

Choosing a Viking sword

A Viking warrior's sword is his most precious, and priciest, weapon. A good sword can take a blacksmith a year to make, so no wonder it costs a fortune. Here are some tips for choosing a top-notch blade:

1 Look for a blade with a **herringbone** pattern. This means it's been made from several iron rods twisted and beaten together to make the blade strong and flexible.

2 Check that the sword is well balanced, with the weight of the **hilt** balancing out the weight of the blade. This will make it lighter and easier to handle.

3 Store your sword in a sheepskin-lined scabbard when it's not in use. This will keep it clean and stop it from getting rusty. A rusty sword's no use to anyone.

Viking Warship

Any Viking raiding party worth its salt needs a **longship**, and we've spent weeks building a new one. It's going to be the best ever: lightning fast, strong, and shallow enough to sail up rivers and land on beaches when we want to launch a surprise attack. It's made of the finest oak and pine—only the best for my dad—and it's around 72 feet (22 meters) long. When it's finished, it'll have a dragon's head carved at the front. I've been practicing rowing in case I need to take my turn at the oars, but there's also a sail for when the wind gets up.

WARNING!

When building a ship, be careful with your tools. You don't want a finger or a toe to fall victim to your hammer.

How to build a longship

First, cut down an oak tree to make the **keel**. Then cut long planks of wood for the sides and shorter planks for the crossbeams and ribs. Each side plank overlaps the one below it to make the ship very strong. Join the pieces together with wooden pegs and iron nails, and stuff any cracks with sheep's wool, dipped in tar, to make the ship watertight.

Tips for navigation

Vikings don't have fancy instruments to help them navigate. You'll mostly have to use your knowledge of the sun, moon, stars, waves, and local landmarks to help you stay on course. Luckily, this is something Vikings are very skilled at.

1 Sail as close to the coast as possible, looking out for landmarks on the shore.

2 During the day, use your sun compass (it's like a sundial). The higher the sun, the farther south you are. The lower the sun, the farther north you are.

3 At night, watch the stars. The polestar always points you to the north.

The ship's going to be pretty crowded, with around fifty of us on board. There's just space to sleep on deck, among the chests of supplies. We've loaded up with bread, sour milk, dried fish, and porridge to eat. Here's hoping I don't get seasick.

Going A-Viking!

Wish I'd never mentioned seasickness. It has been terrible. We set off at dawn the day before last and headed west. At first the weather was good for sailing, with clear skies and a strong wind behind us. In fact, it was really boring, with nothing to do but eat, sleep, and fish. Then a storm blew up . . .

Anyway, we've finally reached northeastern England, where we're going to attack a monastery. My first raid's about to start. The main thing is to get in and out with our loot and prisoners as quickly as we can, and to make my father proud.

Choose the time of year carefully. The best time to go raiding is between April and October. After that, the weather gets really unpredictable and you run the risk of being shipwrecked.

Norway

Sweden

Denmark

England

How to launch a raid

You're within sight of land, and you're armed and ready to raid. Luckily for you, it's foggy, so no one's spotted you, giving you the crucial element of surprise.

1 You run the ship ashore and jump out. Then you haul it up onto the beach.

2 You send an advance party ahead to cover any escape routes.

3 The rest of you attack the monastery. You need to be quick before the monks can send for help.

4 You grab as much treasure as you can and take some of the monks prisoner.

5 Then you set fire to the monastery before heading back to the ship.

Spoils of War

The raid's over, and we're heading for home, before the villagers come after us. We've been busy loading the ships with plunder. We've taken some of the monks prisoner. They'll be sold as slaves when we get back home. It's not a pleasant part of our work, but it's how Vikings make a living. We've also got loads of gold and silver cups and coins, as well as boxes covered in jewels that the monks kept books and holy **relics** in. My father says all this loot will be shared among the raiders, with him getting the biggest share, of course!

Some Vikings bury their loot for safety, always intending to come back later and reclaim their valuables. Some never make it, and rich troves of treasure may be found in the future, buried under farmers' fields. Imagine digging up all that!

How to ransom a hostage

Choose the most important monks to **ransom**. Someone senior, like an abbot, can bring a fortune.

1 Put a price on your hostage. Remember, gold's worth much more than silver.

2 Promise the ransom payer safe passage. You don't want them harmed before you get the cash.

3 Look after any hostages well—unless the ransom isn't paid. Then all bets are off.

4 You can also hold holy objects, books, and relics for ransom. People will pay well to get these treasures back.

WARNING!

Guard your prisoners carefully. If they escape, you can wave good-bye to your profits!

Victory Feast

WARNING!

Don't eat too much at the feast or you might end up breaking your bench!

We're safely back home, and my father's throwing a huge feast to celebrate a successful raid. It's a chance for him to show off how rich (and generous) he is, so there's plenty of food and drink. I'm digging into my third helping of boiled blood pudding. Delicious! Everyone's put on their best clothes and jewelry and crammed into the hall. The feast'll go on for hours, so I might go to bed before the boasting begins . . .

Boasting about how brave and strong you are is an important part of any Viking feast. But don't fall into the trap of boasting about something you can't do. If you brag about taking on the enemy single-handed, make sure you can live up to it. Your honor is at stake.

Writing a poem

The skald (poet) has composed a poem about my father's latest victory. It'd better be good. Here are some top tips for writing your own.

1 Go on a raid yourself. Then you'll know what you're talking about.

2 Talk up the jarl's achievements. Your job is to make him look good.

3 Use lots of fancy-sounding phrases like "weapon storm" for *battle* and "battle sweat" for *blood*.

Bitter Battle

A year's passed since my first raid, and now we're back in Britain, in the far north of Scotland. This time there are a few hundred of us and a fleet of longships. We've come over to fight the Scots and grab some land. My father says he doesn't have enough to give all his sons a decent plot, so he wants to take some from the Scots. But the Scots are fighting back bravely, and at the moment, we're surrounded. The plan is to form a guard around my dad using our shields to make a wall. If he's killed, we're in trouble.

Start looking and sounding like a winner, even before you go into battle. It'll scare your enemy (let's hope). Polish your weapons and armor and make as much noise as you can. Don't forget to pray to Odin. It might not help, but it can't do any harm.

How to fight like a berserker

If you really want to make your mark in battle, become a **berserker**, the wildest Viking warrior of all. Here's what to do:

1 Before battle, work yourself up into a frenzy, howling and biting on your shield.

2 Don't bother with armor. Wear a scary bearskin or wolfskin instead.

3 Fly into a fury as you fight. Worrying about being killed is for wimps.

WARNING!

Bad luck if you're picked as **standard bearer.** You won't be able to defend yourself, so you'll make an easy target for the enemy.

Death of a Warrior

Well, we won the battle in Scotland, but my father was badly wounded. When we got home, we sat by his bedside and prayed to the gods to make him well, but he died last night. Because he was a great chief, we're going to give him a good send-off in his longship with all the things he'll need in the next life: treasure, weapons, food and drink, two of his finest horses, and Ulf, his favorite hunting dog.

Sometimes, ships are buried rather than being set on fire. (An almost perfectly preserved burial ship was found in Norway in 1880. The wet clay had stopped it from rotting. Inside was the body of a king, surrounded by burial goods, including six dogs, twelve horses, and a peacock.)

How to bury a chief

Only the richest and most important Vikings are given a ship burial. Here's how to make sure things run smoothly.

1 Dress the chief in his best clothes and finest jewelry.

2 Place his body in a tent on the deck of his longship.

3 Pack all of his belongings around him.

4 Set the ship on fire.

Most Vikings can't afford a longship. If you're lucky, you might be buried in a small rowing boat or in a grave marked out by stones in the shape of a longship. That's as close as you'll get to the real thing.

Gods of War

It's been a sad time since my father's death, but at least we know that he died a hero. That's the greatest honor for a Viking warrior, and it means that he'll join the band of warriors at Valhalla, Odin's hall in Asgard (the realm of the gods). There, the warriors spend their days practicing their fighting skills and their nights feasting on the finest food and drink. Bet my dad will enjoy that!

Odin is the father of all of the gods. We believe he causes battles by hurling down his magic spear. His magnificent hall, Valhalla (Hall of the Slain) has walls made from golden spears and a roof made from golden shields.When a battle begins, two ravens, Hugin and Munin, report the news to Odin. He sends out the **Valkyries**, female warriors who swoop over the battlefield and decide who will live and who will die. They take the souls of dead heroes and carry them to Valhalla. There's one on the left!

Ragnarok: The Last Battle

Vikings believe there will be a last, great battle, called Ragnarok, which will cause the downfall of the gods and the end of the world. After Ragnarok, Midgard (the land of humans) will freeze over. All humans will be killed, except for one couple. The sun and moon will be eaten by wolves, plunging the world into darkness and chaos. Eventually, a new world will rise up, with a new race of gods and people. We hope!

Ten Vicious Viking Facts

1 The Vikings definitely lived up to their name. The word *viking* comes from an old Norse phrase that means "to go raiding."

2 Vikings fed injured warriors onion soup, then smelled them to see how bad their wounds were. A bad infection would smell stronger than onions!

3 Viking bread was made from flour, water, and so much grit that it wore their teeth down.

4 If you killed another Viking, you had to pay *wergild,* or blood money, to his family.

5 "Never leave your weapons behind when you go to the fields. You may need them" (Viking saying).

6 A Viking's toilet was a hole in the ground, with moss or sheep's wool for toilet paper.

7 Viking leader Ivan the Boneless may have gotten his name because he had such weak legs that his men carried him into battle on a shield.

8 Viking warriors were scared to die in bed in case they went to Niflheim, the underworld.

9 Viking nicknames included "Troll Burster," "Squint-Eyed," "Bent Backwards," and "Foul Fart."

10 Erik the Red, who discovered Greenland, gave the cold island that fine-sounding name to encourage more Vikings to go there.

Glossary

berserker
a warrior transformed and strengthened by battle fury

byrnie
a shirt made from chain mail

herringbone
a pattern made from V-shapes

hilt
the handle of a sword

hird
a group of warriors who fought for a jarl

jarl
a wealthy noble, or earl, in Viking society

keel
the long piece of wood that runs from one end of a ship to the other

longship
a type of wooden ship with cloth sails, invented by Vikings

oath
a solemn and binding promise

ransom
money paid for the safe return of a prisoner or precious object

relic
a holy object, such as the bones or belongings of a saint

skald
a Viking poet

standard bearer
someone who carries a standard (the army's flag) into battle

Valkyrie
a female warrior who carries the souls of dead warriors to Valhalla

INDEX

The Author
Anita Ganeri is an award-winning author of educational children's books. She has written on a huge variety of subjects, from Vikings to viruses and from Romans to world religions. She was born in India and now lives in England with her family and pets.

The Artist
Mariano Epelbaum was born in Buenos Aires, Argentina. He grew up drawing and looking at small insects under the stones in the garden of his grandmother's house. He has worked as an art director and character designer for many films in Argentina and Spain.